Breaking the Sickle:

A Snippet of the Life of Dr. Yvette Fay Francis-McBarnette

Written By: Louie T. McClain II
Edited By Francis W. Minikon Jr.
Illustrated by: M. Ridho Mentarie

T0027326

Melanin Origins

1

This bond that we have can never be broken.

I learned at a very young age that love and friendship is shown by helping the ones that you care about the most.

But still, being a true blessing to all involves helping absolute strangers too.

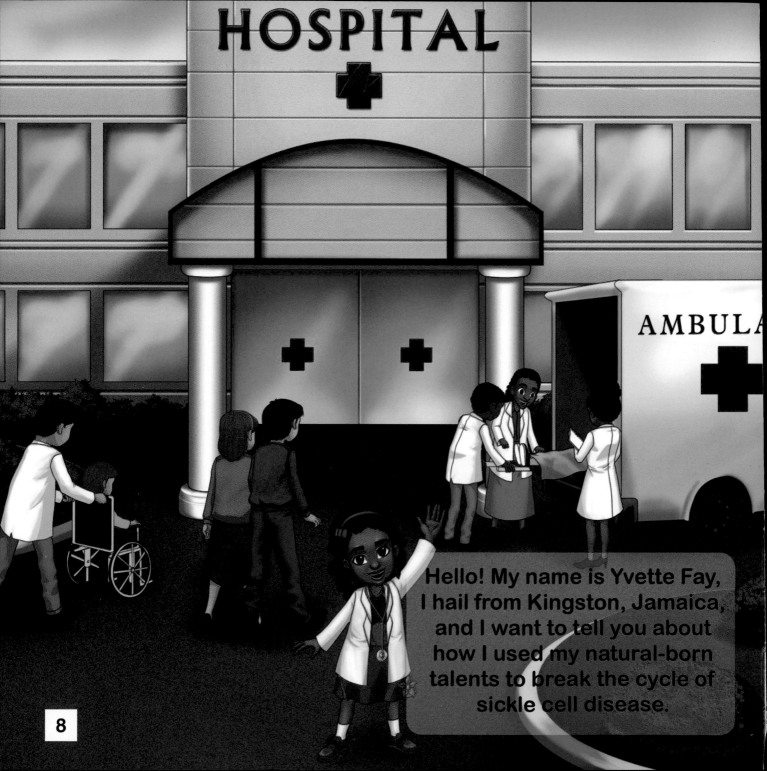

Imagine the word "cycle" as the shape of a circle. On this circle, good and bad things keep happening over and over again.

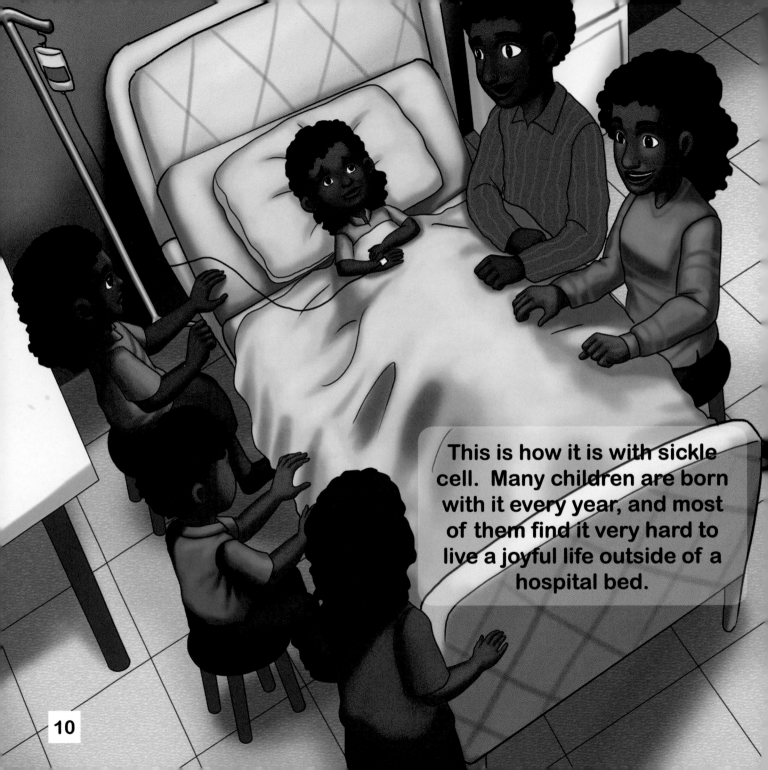

This is how it is with sickle cell. Many children are born with it every year, and most of them find it very hard to live a joyful life outside of a hospital bed.

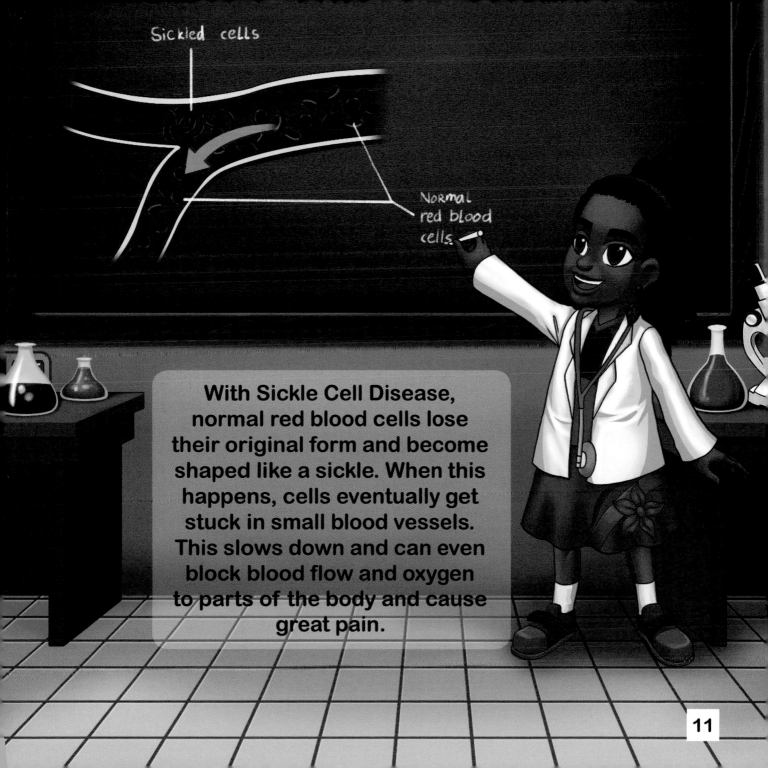

Sickled cells

Normal red blood cells

With Sickle Cell Disease, normal red blood cells lose their original form and become shaped like a sickle. When this happens, cells eventually get stuck in small blood vessels. This slows down and can even block blood flow and oxygen to parts of the body and cause great pain.

I never knew of sickle cell until I did some work at the hospital in Chicago and I saw firsthand how it affected people's lives.

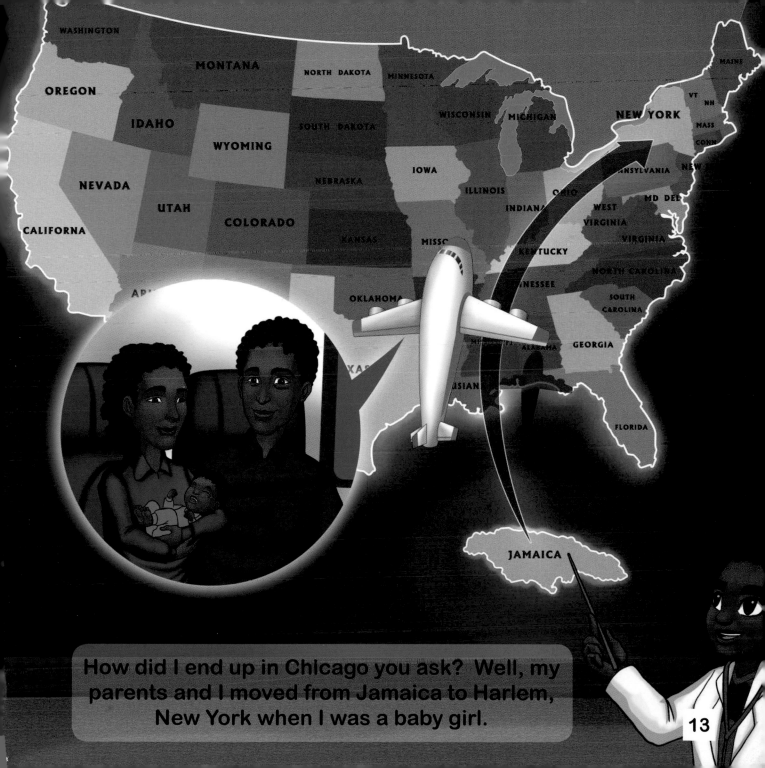

How did I end up in Chicago you ask? Well, my parents and I moved from Jamaica to Harlem, New York when I was a baby girl.

13

Every day I honored my mother and my father by reading books, doing my chores, and making good grades in school.

14

I really believe that trying your best pays off, because I was only 19 years old when I was started school at Yale University's School of Medicine.

15

It was my study of medicine that led me to the great city of Chicago,

and it was in Chicago that I made up my mind that I was going to do something to break the cycle!

17

Sickle cell is a blood disorder that causes great pain in your body,

shortness of breath

As a doctor of medicine, I knew that I had to do something to ease the pain and help those who were suffering,

So I moved back to New York City and decided to make a difference in people lives.

I learned people can feel better and have more energy if they took the right medicines each day.

Also, when babies were born, I made sure their parents brought them to my office so I can make sure everything was alright.

If a child was born with sickle cell, I made sure their parents had everything that they needed to take good care of their baby.

The work that I did was able to touch so many lives that the President of the United States of America put me in charge of a team that would help every person with sickle cell in the entire country.

and having a heart to help others in need brings about the best blessings in life.

For this is the bond of unity with the human race.

29

More Information:

Sickle Cell Disease is an inherited blood disorder that mostly affects people of African ancestry, but also occurs in other ethnic groups, including people who are of Mediterranean and Middle Eastern descent. It is reported that approximately 200,000 Americans have Sickle Cell Disease.

25% of all proceeds from this book will be donated to The Sickle Cell Disease Association of North Texas to help fund research to cure Sickle Cell Disease and enhance the quality of life of people living with the disease across the world. Additional information can be found at www.scdatarrant.org